Don

Down the Lane

For my friends

First published in 2008 by
DEADGOOD Publications
England

Copyright © Don Walls 2008. All rights reserved. No part of this publication may be reproduced, stored in a retrieval system, or transmitted, in any form or by any means, without the prior permission of the author.

Cover illustration by Don Walls

Also by Don Walls:
"In the Shed", published in 2005 (ISBN 0-9546937-1-X)
"Inside Out", published in 2006 (ISBN 0-9546937-4-4)

Printed by Abbey Print, Hemingbrough, North Yorkshire, England

CONTENTS

Uncle Ted (Window Cleaner)	1
Scarborough	2
The Baker	3
Quail	4
My Mother	5
I make magic through little things	6
By the Line	7
My Father's Watch	8
Black and White	9
Fish and Chips	10
My Sister	11
Young girls smile at me	12
My Mother and Mrs Trotter	13
For Tom - Steeplejack	14
Starlings	15
Tippex	16
Aspects of my Toes	17
For William - Wood Carver	18
Ken	19
My Father	20
Aunt Edie	21
The Horse	22
The Cobbler's Shop	23
A Spade's a Spade...	24
Gossip	25
Doctor	26
We were close together in terrace houses in the War	27
For Mary	28
For Peter	29
Fear	30
Belly	31
My Praying Mantis	32
Seals off Hilbre Island	33
Glance	34
Plumber	35
Tom the Dustbin Man	36
Politics	37

CONTENTS (continued)

In Memoriam	38
For Paul (Bricklayer)	39
exam	40
Teenager	41
On meeting an old soldier who would not buy a poppy	42
Moss	43
For Moira	44
Elephant	45
Snow	46
Poem	47
Bed	48
How to keep a Crow	49
Zebra	50
Language and Forgetfulness	51
Swifts	52
David	53
Imagery	54
Chocolate Suit	55
Goat	56
Owl	57
The Autumn Nightingale	58
Bottles	59
Resolution	60
Tiger	61
Skin	62
John	63
Linda	64
I'd been in this head for seventy years	65
Shopping with Mary	68
Hippo	69
Wildebeest	70-71
Mary's Canary	72
Tracking the elusive elephants with Mary at night in the City of York	73
The Whale, Crystal Therapy and Mary	74
Crocodile	75
For Christmas Mary bought me a didgeridoo	76

Uncle Ted (Window Cleaner)
(For Antonia and Steve)

The ladder
- half-way up
he'd stop to light up,
stretched to his limits
his life a balance of buckets and fags.

He knew every house
the geometry of dormers
the angles of gossip
- why Linda Lane had gone away
to stay with Grandma in farest Kent,
the slippery winters
on the rungs,
on glass the sun
blinding, bright
and what was wobbly down the street
- half-truths, rumours,
no foothold in fact,

and his bird's-eye view
of plants on the sills
chattering starlings
and from a word in the wind
sadness, love
and gravity
the reality of where he stood
the slant of shadows over the roofs
the hypotenuse of evening light
and the topmost rung
and his space in the world,
the song of birds
a leaf in the wind.

Scarborough

To Scarborough on a train
- tea and lettuce sandwiches
and chunks of chocolate cake
deep and dark for the teeth to sink into,
the happy smoke and manic wheels,
fields unfolding,

the harbour:
fish - thousands of eyes staring back
silver stippled decks
and nets already drying
for tomorrow's catch
- sea fret, darkness
and the boom of boats
booming as far as Dogger Bank,
and I wished they'd boom for ever and ever,
gulls and spray
the great arc of the bay
- pebbling, crabbing
and somewhere behind us the tides rushing in
- gullies, pools
and the strange excitement of the sea all around us.

The Baker
(For Carol and Paul)

The family lived above the shop
their father the master baker,
his wife and daughters
- flour and yeast
water salt
and the measure of heat
air and cooling
and the warmth of bread
golden, plump
at the oven's mouth,
embers dying

and the time for tea
crusts and dripping
whiffs of cinnamon
sesame seeds,
laughter banter
and then the sister
who never came back
the cold of winter
hawthorns, aspens
heavy with snow
- the days the dough
mists of flour and the family
warming at the oven's mouth.

Quail

We learnt about creatures great and small
the sparrow that falls,
and so one day we picked up a quail on Clifton Ings,
stunned in snow.
We stroked its neck
and warmed it close
- a speckled bird the size of a fist.
I'd heard it in the bracken, heather,
a call like 'wet my lips, wet my lips.'

Spring, a flock of them blown off course on Clifton Ings,
wings exhausted -
'Manna from heaven,' my uncle said and wrung their necks
- this little bird that crossed the steppes
over the hills and peaks of air
- a tiny bundle of feathers, bones.
I picked one up.
Head streaked white, it craned its neck
a glint of a question in its eyes.

Finger and thumb round its neck,
'Just hold it like this and pull,' my uncle said.

Click.

My Mother

The smell of cocoa down the lane
- white waves of women coming home
and among them my mother.
Her kitchen and the happy sounds
- all talking together
flavours, stirrings
and my mother singing
and for my father a mug of tea, a hug
- tiredness dissolving.

Always Lent
and my sister and I shared an egg
and my mother nowt
'til dad came home friday nights
then both of them spouting
- the unfairness of things
and my mother's voice
and women's rights
and women could do owt
that men could do
but women were nowt
downtrodden, doormats
and she loosened dad's boots
then came upstairs
and tucked us in.

Snowdrops she loved - their pale heads.
Her delight in yellow - primrose
aconite, violets on the North York Moors
and all summer long
the Ings together
and once a year a day on the beach
and my mother splashed my sister and me
and we splashed back
and ran and laughed
and so did she,
my mother as daft as my sister and me.

I make magic through little things:
these grasses dried and stirred in the draught
as I open the door.
You could not press enough of them.
And the jottings you left:
loops of your voice,
your glass in the fire-glow
- a dapple of planets. Space
you loved,
here in this photograph,
small in the whiteness,
the mystery of snow.

By the Line
(For Dick Hunter)

Us kids, Shirty White and Mick and Me
- every night by the line
warping in moonlight,
the gravelly clinkers
- sleepers, sun and ice
woodlice, moss
and we placed our ha'pennies on the tracks
and waited
then the song of the line
and out of the mist
the roaring train
and the rush of wind, steam and smoke
windows and the yellow lights
and us in the weeds
- glimpses
a smile, a grimace
a bowler hat
hands speaking
and the shadows passing.
The song of distance,
Mick and Me and Shirty White.

My Father's Watch

Often I take out my Father's watch
thumbed and polished.
The whiteness of its face
and the black certainty
the numbers claim.
The minutiae of time
- the second hand
and I count the ticks:
how long it takes
from flash to thunderclap
or to hold my breath
and the minute hand - twelve o'clock already
and I look again
five past - twenty past
and where have the minutes gone?

His watch in my hand
- the closeness of things,
the hour hand
which never seems to move
yet the days slip by
- loves, laments.

Black and White

Made ice cream
swept chimneys
played the piano and sang.

Sundays, swathes of keys
whites and flats
pianissimo, crescendo,
the clatter of canes for the massive sweeping.
The sad music of blackness
- the white dove dead, halfway up. The bat.
The suffocating soot.
and once in my mother's whitewashed kitchen
the backblast, the black mist
and we came out running
eyes burning,
and he never stopped singing
brush bristling in the morning light
- starlings, crows.

The black magician
opening the door on New Year's Eve,
songs and weddings
ice cream
and the bogeyman
chasing us down the snowlanes.

Fish and Chips

out of the Press Friday nights
fresh air, appetites
and my mother excited
read the names of the newly dead
hovering over one she knew
- now existing, now not -
and my father's face puckered at front page news:
killed in action, Jews in France. His tic.
He stabbed the chips
and attacked the haddock.
My sister's glance
as I stuffed my gob with batter and skin
and still enough mouth for back page sport
- York's win at Wigan, Stockport
and other news a waste of space:
politics, weddings
and I scoured the print
for scraps of scandal.
My mother squinted
at my tastes.

Friday nights in the street
- banter, icy feet
and the warming glance over black print
on a cold night.

My Sister

She rings every week
- the same lament:
grabbing, greed
and all the sadness of getting ahead.
So many beliefs
- numbers dead

and how little things matter
- the stray dog on the beach
birds on the sill
goldfinch, thrush
and cows stepping close
their large brown eyes, curious, sad,
the lessening of light
and the bees disappear
and over the years
the lovely eccentrics down the lane
frosts, cold freshness
and all that snow
to be trodden yet.

Young girls smile at me
as I walk through the market
over Ouse bridge.
White hair helps
baldness and a crumpled face
and once a verruca distorted my gait
and smiles lit up the streets of York
from Bootham Bar to Melrosegate,
so I practised a limp
and found looking vacant
lost or sad
a useful strategy for kindling concern
at checkouts in Tescos, M & S.

My Mother and Mrs Trotter
(For Chris and Peter)

Words to and fro over the wall
- my mother and Mrs Trotter
in sun and drizzle,
my mother proud of my school report
Mrs Trotter her son
and I listened and learnt about myself
perspectives I'd never seen before
- ambitions,
then all the gossip down the lane
and my mother's voice
the lilt of joy
intonations of sadness,
Mrs Trotter, my mother
wooly clad in snow,
in summer 'til the moon came round
laughter for the world to know,
whisperings
and quieter still the language of hands.
The closeness on a winter's night.

For Tom - Steeplejack

High buildings round the city
towers, steeples
blackbirds and shadows,
the history of footholds
and shades of builders
blocks and tackle
moss
- greenness, greyness
ropes and ladders and keeping a balance
- false steps in the wind
the view of the world, sheer and angled,
mists and moods
shaping stones
the shrill language of starlings.
Daddy longlegs, swifts.

Starlings
(For Emily and Ben)
(selected from a previous publication)

The starlings were dying. We didn't know why.
We found two beneath the laurel - freshly dead,
the sheen of life on their feathers still.
We put them in shoe boxes.

On the wireless everyday George V,
lying in state. Soldiers by his catafalque.
Long glum queues. We wondered what he looked like dead,
wearing his pyjamas.

The starlings. It was their silence surprised us most.
All the din in the hawthorn tree,
singing with wings partly open.
Once they mobbed a crow. On the lawn stabbed.

We thought of George V jolted round London in his gun carriage.
All day my parents listened to the wireless. Dead music,
and the newspaper came - sheets of it. Black.
His life in the navy.

At Windsor he was buried in the vaults.
He'd last longer there, we thought.
We'd learnt about the Pharoahs and mummification,
lead and gold coffins.

For burial we wrapped the starlings in flags the size of handkerchiefs,
then thought that a waste of flags
and lay them straight into the grave we'd dug
- glints of blue, green, red in the afternoon sun.

We made mimic bugles with our hands and played the last post.

Tippex

My Mother said I was addicted early on,
not to its smell but its ability to annihilate words
so I practised on comics - Beano, Dandy -
and by the age of ten was tippexing whole libraries out of existence.
Then, started my white offensive against all irritations -
History, teachers, Geography, Maths.
I stockpiled it in the pantry.
It whitewashed anything into oblivion
(a man could even use it on himself).
So I included pollution and famine in the white-out,
also black fear,
but you have to be careful not to smudge love.
Now I'm planning a blizzard against wars and politicians -
they should be buried in drifts of it.
If I start on the latter first, it will cost less in Tippex.

Aspects of my Toes

They have taken a vow of silence,
obedient as monks in the nave of my shoes
- prostrate in darkness.
Shoeless at night they savour the carpet,
adore the dark freedom of my bed.
Curious, emerge beyond the sheets
- primeval,
a work of Art in gracelessness,
vandals in socks.
On the frontiers of sleep
I hear them marching across the steppes.

For William - Wood Carver

He could see inside the wood he carved
and followed the grain
whorls and knots
rivulets, mounds
and he'd chisel and plane
into the mystery of the dark
releasing the grace of bird and deer
beneath his palm for closeness sake.

Ken

I was ten and he already dead - the diptheria epidemic 38-39
and I stopped kicking the ball against the shed
trapped it between my legs
the family arriving,
church and prayers
easing death

and I stood for days
stunned in Spring
the soundless ball
between my legs,
and from the touchline of the years
I see him still
in greenness, whiteness
swerve the ball across the field
bouncing faithfully at my feet.

My Father

His ramshackle bike
- freewheeling home,
I met him in the tired light,
his cap on my head
and we talked of fishing in sun and ice.
Some nights he'd sit in the backyard shed
'til the starlings chattered.

Friday nights, happy, well-oiled
he fumbled the sneck on the backyard door,
his pay packet plundered
and to make it right
dry-gobbed he'd go for a week or more.

He mimicked the boss
wallowing in vowels of the upper class
and touched his cap
us writhing on the kitchen floor,

and then he'd spout:
the working man's nowt,
democracy's shite
- open your gob
and you lose your job
and no-one dare mention the Jarrow Strike.
Every day dripping and bread
and for my dad the staff of life
a woodbine bobbing in his gob.
His allotment by the Scarborough line,
we'd tig and run
between the beans and garden peas
his leeks maturing in shit and sun.

Snooker King of the Working Men's Club
we fished the Ings for pike and chub
and you could tell by his eyes
wildness was the gift of life.

Bath nights, he'd lift me up to the kitchen mirror
smothered white
and from my cheeks he'd blow the suds
snowflakes floating over us.

Aunt Edie

Aunt Edie's house
- Sundays dropping in
red roses, laughter
and we'd clap and sing
auntie Edie on the piano,
cold drinks
and all of us walked the Ings together
and down the street
her hand on my shoulder
- her listening eyes
and my latest obsessions of the week
- aeroplanes, trains
spiders, flies
and like my mam and auntie May
she never stopped to chat to neighbours
- me on the edge of endless talk,
and when my father died
she sat by the coffin
and stroked his head
and talked of the years,
her door wide open
to friends, relations
and then the stranger from the new estate
and whisperings drifted down the street
and then I learnt what nudging meant
in the Co-op, the corner shop,
and she bought me sweets
lollipops,
cough drops.

The Horse

We loved to see the wash of pee
deep yellow, pungent
its lingering smell
and we fetched grass and vetch
and patted his neck
combed his back patient in rain.
What a horse he was!
- mane and tail
fetlocks, clip clop
and once we sang to him.
He neighed.

Late November, eyes blood red
he collapsed in the lane
- the blaze on his head
my bucket and spade,
the steaming gold.

The Cobbler's Shop

Shoes everywhere
scuffed,
imprints of toes
and a hundred expressions of myself
- the inner uncertainty
wobbly on ice
- risks and chance
the wrong road taken
and the long way back
- arid in Greece
and sodden in Spring
greenness, squelchings,
soles worn thin,
and explorations never cease:
shale, moss
and the sea coming in
- shoes kicked off.

A Spade's a Spade...

Walking in the park with Grandad,
'Mind the shit', my little son said.

Grandad stepped aside amazed,
not at the shit, at what he said.

'Don't say that, say filth or dirt'.
'Then how'll you know it's shit,' he said.

Gossip

Gossip in church, back lanes
as far away as Newborough Street,
the morning ladling of the milk
mothers and prams
and behind lace curtains
hides
observing closeness in the dark,
whisperings
the meaning of smiles,
a glance
the language of hands

and gossip never burnt itself out
rekindled by words
- out of wedlock, shame
and apostasy of any kind:
how to raise ferrets
bring up kids
and like an animal gossip came down the lane
sniffing, nosing things out
never letting things go.

Doctor

The surgery
- another world
permanganate - blood red
pee-yellows, vein blues
the throb of fear
and the intonation of his voice
just as if I wasn't there,
a dominance that spread to everything
- all the instruments for blood and probing
and listening to the deadly lungs
and he placed an 'aa' spoon
on my tongue
and I was afraid.

My father's depression
- his tic
and the chill between them,
my mother ill
and we waited for days
then he blustered in,
my father unleashing swarms of words
I'd only heard on Friday nights
when the pubs turned out.
Words that puckered the doctor's brow
and made us cringe

and we didn't have a doctor
for weeks on end.

We were close together in terrace houses in the War.
Come the 50s, we moved to semis:
no longer blunt and back-lane mouthed
our verbs, taboo,
burst inside the house.
'Bugger it,'
we missed the terrace.

Semis - borders pretty, but frontiers still
weeds the enemy, true gardeners
squinted over the hedge
at where our vetch and chickweed grew,
golden grasses.

Recently, there's a drifting back
to terraces among the younger folk
- a kind of intellectual, existential lot,
a bouncy Citroen at the door,
inside selected wines, guitars.
Not the terraces we knew
with the edge of the world two streets away
- coronations, jubilees
and sitting out nights in gossip gangs.
England at Headingley in back lane cricket.

I've lived in this semi for twenty years
and have never seen
(judging from the lawns, shaved bald)
those dustless sanctuaries of neighbours' inner homes.
Everywhere privet
and along the backs conservatories spread.

For Mary

A few sauces, condiments, two candles herald eating
and in the kitchen some mystery going on:
the clink of spoon and knife
dishes shifting,
stirrings,
and I pay homage to smells
tonight Greek - appetites rekindled
- Corinth, Athens,
warmth spilling over and filling the house.

We travel in flavours:
Anatolian kebabs, Moroccan lamb,
the glow of wine.
We tear off pieces from the same warm loaf.

For Peter

On the beach in the morning light
we follow the tide
- pebbles, shells,
the stillness of pools
and the roaring darkness out at sea
flecks of gulls
oystercatchers in the wind
and at our feet the speckled stones
- pebbles smooth for the palms of our hands,
the sea coming in
ammonites, rocks
and you ahead where sand and water briefly meet
and the guillemots feed.

Fear

I learnt about fear early on.
It thrived on the thought of being found out
- they could take you away for throwing stones, saying damn.

Some fears grabbed me by the scruff of the neck -
at five, under the tap they held my head.
Execution by water - face up.

At seven when my Mother was ill I stood at the door.
Sheets of blood stuffed the bin.

At ten the Airdale snarled and threatened my throat.
I never took papers round again.

For days sometimes a fear lay low
then suddenly swooped out of the darkness of my head,
even in Spring with its blossom and birdsong.

It hovered overhead,
a fear exuding a clammy unease, unseating bowels.
It never pounced this kind of fear. It stalked

- shoulder blades rolling in the long Summer grass.
'Face it,' my elders said. I faced it then fled.
By the age of eleven I sat in my mind and watched it pass.

Belly

As a boy it was not the belly
but the belly-button that claimed attention
- a fascinating squiggle with its mystery of purpose,
but not until the hair hell-bent on retreat
and the teeth were sleeping in steradent
did the belly itself claim recognition,
peering barefaced over my waist.
I heaved it in
and on my back raised my legs,
my thighs incensed,
but as for my belly, it was not impressed.
I heard it chuckling.

No snacks, sweets,
only grapefruit which puckers my mouth with citric acid
and the boredom of sameness
and the affirmation of my wife of the high repute
of grapefruit in diet.

As a boy the only world I knew was the world rushing forward
- a kind of truth round the next corner
though now the truth is where I am
as I view myself in the bedroom mirror
- arms and legs thin as sticks
neck like a turkey
and the bulge of my belly,
refusing to budge.

My Praying Mantis
(For Liz and Martin)

She sits and prays,
what her religion is I cannot say.
Her favourite colour's green,
so I walk her on baize,
praise her
as one might praise a dog or a cat.

Still for days,
but feed her greenfly, ant or gnat
voracious gobbles
then sits and prays
in praise of what I cannot say,

and once on my shoulder the smaller male
cautiously made love to her
then she swallowed him whole
- lover and prey -
and sat and prayed.
What her religion is I cannot say.

Seals off Hilbre Island
(In memory of A)

First sighting an age ago
- three seals flopped on the beach.
We walked towards them
lolloping in the surf,
riding the waves out to sea.
Three heads glistening.

Ten summers ago
I found a cowrie shell for her collection
offered her pebbles
- fresh reds and blues.
We were being watched.
Three heads, wide eyed in the wash and spray,

and today alone I walk the bay of Hilbre Island
and the sea is still
- a few syllables on rocks -
then an eddy, a rippling
and out of the greyness
three heads glistening.

Glance

This glance belongs to my wife
more eloquent than speech
unsettling my belly
feet,
and cornered sometimes
I dare to glance back
her eyes half closed, nose in the air
the shrug, the stare
eyeing my shoes,
the half-smile to confuse.

Plumber

Hacksaw, cold chisel
lead and lagging
and skills passed on
- annealing, welding
and drawn out long
his Yorkshire speech
his blowlamp roaring,
the magic of heat.
Gunge released in sinks and drains
unblocking smiles
and folk dropping in
to view the 40's lovely lav, its generous waters.
Whatever gurgled in the loft
- the stopcock.

His world a world of folk and things
tittle tattle down the lane
trickles swelling, floods, burst pipes
the fusion of metals
births and weddings,
gravity and the flow of things
- the plumbline, the spirit level.

Tom the Dustbin Man

Every Friday he emptied the bins
rancid fats
ash
shells and kippers
sea bass, cats
- the texture of the past,
stains, toenails,
pearly buttons on a blouse,
ribbons frayed
and beautiful once
dead flowers plants
the thrush on its back
grappling the air
shreds of love
- letters cards,
chicken bones, socks,
sequins in a world of rot.

Politics

Cold war was something we learned early on -
long cold feuds of

not talking to Auntie May and Uncle Len,
weathering silence for months on end

'til detente grew on neutral ground
of funerals, weddings ...

then we'd all band together
against Auntie Vi and Uncle Ben.

In Memoriam

I sat on the bench
behind me the plaque:
two students - the crash
in '76 on the way to Zagreb
and the shock of chance
my friends, the Lanes
on the self same flight,
and late at night
the phone
and sounds of names shaping faces
a smile
a glance
the smell of his pipe
her eyes.
Vapour trails across the skies.

For Paul (Bricklayer)

He lays the foundation
- something certain
for what the years might bring.
Then the first bricks, the wall
facing the rain, the sun
scaffolding
and balancing at the chimney breast
gables
and the sky a world of clouds and crows
the nature of things
gravity, gaps
the bedraggled wind
and nothing in itself complete:
lintels, beams
floorboards - joists
and beneath facades
- pebbledash, cladding -
the firmness of bricks,
the sounds of magic:
purlins, mullions
crazy paving and leaded lights
and quietly at night
the furtive shadows,
the slant of roofs.
The morning sun in wetness.

exam

then they sat us down
and me with all those
butterflies like in my stomach
separate in desks
and cells of time
that is forty minutes
to write on some lousy topic
that only interested them that set it
and me trying to get all serious
so I'd write well
with moistening palms and
pushing out the thought of what I'd
do after the exam because
the minutes were dripping away
and I had to get
some crap down
but got into that
like always under pressure
what does it matter anyway
philosophical knot
I only untied with a
join the absurdity you silly bugger
which is how
most of my life I have managed to pass

Teenager

She plucks her eyebrows out,
then paints them on again.
Hair - copper beech, ponytail,
lips - red rose, nails,
threadbare jeans,
eyeshadow - green.
A diamante on her belly
and one on her nose
anti teachers,
anyone close.

Surprise! She went with us to Pen-y-Ghent
fetched cowslips, vetch
and then her phone - fluent in lingo:
wicked and cool, everything crap
and I never know where I'll glimpse her next
outside Ziggy's
or hiding where the campion grows.
Her head in the shadows.

On meeting an old soldier who would not buy a poppy
(311 men were executed in the First World War for desertion. Death warrants were signed by Haig whose name was stamped on the black metal centre of the poppy.)

I was walking with him on the barren land by the railway line
poppies everywhere - a billowy redness,
at their deepest in greenness.

'Poppies, poppies,' he said,
then talked of Paschendale, the Somme.
'It was all mud. A hail of mud
and the only greenness, the greenness of gas.
Mortars, sniper cracks. Fire and shrapnel.
The platoon in shreds
and some deranged jabbed and thrust
and cursed the Hun,
shells bursting
and he, mumbling to himself, ran off.
It could have been anyone of us.'

'Poppies, poppies,' he said, 'I never look a poppy in the face.
Its dark centre.'

Moss
(For Ruth and Steve)

It has fetched history with it
and spreads: a quiet accretion
into the next millennium.

Communing with relics
the graveyards are ancient
with its green inscriptions -

it listens to stones,
forming easy accommodations
with walls, trees,

its relationships total,
no dumb neglect
of the humblest ground

which it gently owns,
but never owned
loses nothing. Velvet

and full of goodwill
for sitting on,
even uprooted
it never complains,

its philosophy eastern
it waits
tranquilly certain
spreading like centuries.

For Moira
who suffered from dementia in her later life

I was ten
and she wove her hair
with heather and ling
and walked the moors
- Kirby to Kilburn - the Pennine Way
and where the sheltered flowers grew
Roseberry Topping
- owls and shrews.

I was twenty-five
and she roamed the lanes
in wind and snow
the sodden Ings
frozen in frost
and we warmed her hands.

Gilamoor
- no memory of curlew
whirr of grouse
fox and hare
nor who we were.
We wove her hair
with heather and ling.

Elephant

The second largest mammal that lives in my head
is the elephant,
but you can't keep an elephant in your head all the time,
the world's too cramped.
So I let him roam on the lawn outside.
He leans against the privet hedge.
My neighbours scowl.

Most of all he likes water and mud
- my head is full of squelchings and squirtings.
Wild at times, my wife calms him down
with stories of the Serengeti.
She strokes his trunk.
He trumpets and rolls,
steps over me gently.

Snow

To understand
one must know the philosophy of snow:
owning nothing
knows neither solitude
nor winter loss
and never clings like ice.
Submits to the wind's will.
Overnight
settles gently,
then moves on.

Poem

I perceive a shape in the mist ahead,
grope for imagery
to find the way forward.

The rhythm may help
and cadence, overflowing from line to line.
Often no foothold,

I cling where I can
testing the strength of mountain plants,
or lost in a forest

as darkness falls
I embrace trunks, heed
the crackle of twigs.
Somewhere there's meaning.

I follow sounds:
nightjar, owl
distant sheep.
A brightness grows beyond the hills,

a poem away.

Bed

The soft hours
stretching - angles, legs,
the smell of starch on my mother's sheets
whiteness, plump pillows
and the head sinking in,
blankets quilts
rills and valleys, snow and lapwings
and the body shifting
this way that
and the feet staring back
the bedclothes slipping
sheets and blankets on the floor
- searching for answers in the dark,
the straightening
the starting again
and the sudden awakening
and nothing where it ought to be
the windows, the door
and where I am.

How to keep a Crow

Sit next to him on the rooftop.
Caw.
Act gawky in a drizzle of rain.
Warm yourself by the chimney stack.
Relax.
Learn the slow flap
and have a day out in the countryside.
Amble in the radiant wheat.

Share stories
- scraps of life
and he'll tell you about his darker side
his low esteem,
so remind him he can walk and hop
use his beak to probe and eat
and show surprise
at the weight of his blackness taking off,
sheen in the sun.

Zebra

I keep a Zebra in my head
he lives in a world of black and white
loves badgers, magpies
penguins, pandas
Newcastle fans
and late at night
sits by the piano and licks the coldness of the keys.
His favourite films - black and white
Chaplin, Mae West
but what he likes best
- barcodes
at Tescos.

Language and Forgetfulness

First proper nouns
lost in the Ocean of Forgetfulness
and no amount of trawling can bring them back,
then common ones too,
washed away in the outgoing tides.
The life-line paraphrasing or resorting to stealth
- on the edge of conversations we lie in wait
'til someone says Jim
and then we join in:
'Jim this, Jim that,' as though we'd known him all along,
and already the future's flooding in
- a few words like limpets clinging still,
syntax grounded
and verbs breaking off like icebergs in Antartica,
some scraps marooned like 'is' and 'and'.
Then the rockets of language in distress
sh ... sh ... sh ... shit
sh ... sh ... sh ... shit
over the Ocean of Forgetfulness.

Swifts
(For Kay and John)

Early May and the swifts are back
so I resume my lessons.
They teach me to relax on air
loop, swoop
inspect eaves
and from the summit of a cloud
I sky-ski down
over the roof tops, manic, shrill,
hoarse with shrieking.
Swifts are geometers of curves
and teach me hyperbolas, circles, ellipses
but I need more practice and somehow lack speed.
They sleep on air.
Also they fornicate in flight.
Now this requires skill.
My girlfriend will not learn to fly.

David

At the Centre she used to visit him.
Her eyes - sunlight on dark water
and they'd look at his book on angling:
small fish - Miller's Thumb, Stone Loach - scales invisible,
dace of the fast waters and sparkling grayling,
predatory perch and zander, tench
and the silver curves of bream and salmon
and he knew which way each fish would swim
- upstream, down, into the depths - shadows,
and he taught her how to cast - hyperbolas, ellipses
and how to reel in - the line taut, gleaming,
lest the fish swim off into the darkness.
His hand on her shoulder.

Sometimes I see him fishing from the quay
and watch him at his skill, sinking the bait,
the bobbing of the float.
He tells me of a sea trout this far upstream,
flashes of silver.

Imagery

I thought I'd write a poem for her
so I rummaged my mind for something rare

an image transcending her present state,
tongue removed and more ops left

to implant radioactive sticks
which would arrest the bastard thing

flowing down the lymph glands.
Bloody likely as barbed wire stopping mist.

Overnight her face took on the lampshade texture of a Belsen Jew
her hair in wisps. Her arms were sticks.

No image transcended this.

Chocolate Suit

I have a chocolate suit
coat dark, trousers milk
comfortable to wear
gives slightly at my body's warmth,
temperature, of course, a gnawing concern:
in a heatwave a chocolate shock
viscid pools in the market, in the bank,
freezing - cumbersome armour,
hard to put on.
I never go to Lapland,
nor Africa in Summer,
and I check the weather every day
- you've got to -
everything could melt away, harden,

but whatever the weather it's all a risk:
walking with pride in my chocolate suit
past Maxwell and Kennedy - chocolate makers of high repute
I got knocked down, got up unscathed
but the chocolate suit in smithereens
kids eyeing the pieces
- the chocolate nightmare I'd always feared:
me in my underwear walking home
- Parliament Street, St. Samson's Square.

Goat

I dreamed of keeping a goat in the backyard shed
- a snow-white goat nibbling carrots
and I would walk him on the Ings
and call him by name,
hide
and he would nuzzle me in the long grass
skip and bleat
reach willows, washing
- always on the edge of what we'd do next.

So, 'Dad,' I said
'can I keep a goat in the backyard shed
- a milk-white goat?'
he shook his head.
'Neighbours and smell, byelaws,' he said
- and all the practicalities of the world
blunting joy,
and love.

Owl

I survive by stealth
songless hide.
Sort out shadows
crinkle of leaves,
whatever pretends to be what it's not
and what I do best - swoop and grab
rive and rend - mouse and vole,
clamp
swallow whole.
In darkness
unearthly
vowel the night.

The Autumn Nightingale

I make my way to the spot I knew
where the roses grew
before the buildings and bulldozers came
where the wire grows barbed in Autumn rain
and the Ministry's planted a sign or two
'Private! Thou shalt not enter,' so I do
searching for the trees I knew
- hornbeam, lime, beech and yew
and a few are left, perhaps the same,
so I huddle and wait for the nightingale.

Bottles

We have our charm,
smooth and graceful,
chilled for the palm in Benidorm.

But you've seen us broken,
white, ethnic - greens and browns.
Work and the scrap heap
there is no race.

Our plastic cousins are gaining ground,
upstart cartons.
In the old days they would take us back.

It's an empty life.

Resolution

Another promise with the thread come loose
(I should never have made it anyway).
Cut it with the scissors and let it be gone.
    I don't care a thimble
    I don't care a pin,
I'll go around in tatters and burst at the seams
but, I'll never be bound by a promise again.

Tiger

I keep a tiger in my head.
Often we play.
If you keep a tiger in your head
you've got to play or it's all too solemn,
so we gambol and roll
and he growls a growl - a soft throated growl,
but it's not all play - he teaches Yoga
- how to turn in less than your length
denying bones.
He's an expert in stealth
and disavows his presence by stalking.
But I never can tell when his moods will change.
Often he's gentle
but no sooner relaxed in the mottled shade
than nosing the air, basso profondo he roars a roar for the stars to know.
I hide in the shadows and watch him pass.

Skin

I wash with it on,
its fashion perennial.
It fits everything: lips, chin.
It's fussy about clothes
and will not wear a nylon shirt, socks,
and hates most of all a puckered crotch.

I cannot take it off.
I go to bed in it,
get up in it
wear it for work and Sunday best,
and over the years there's more of it:
belly, balding
- my head a plateau of it.

But it knows what it likes:
lingering in the bath
fondling after a shave
and most of all your fingers walking over it.

John

He played and sang
at coronations, jubilees
or just for friends
in wind and rain
- for dancing folk along the lane
his imagination bright in lyrics
the song of the aspens - heavy in snow
a leaf in the wind
and the ordinary glowed - the closeness of things.

Linda

Child bearing child:
pregnant again, and why not?
Your vocation's keeping Spring the year round,
with pups and sapling things, your children
and your childlike self,

tremulous and bounding off
at thoughts and sounds -
I never know if you're foal or mare!
Both somehow - mother
and your childlike self,

with pregnancy your bloom of love
for all that scampers grows and sings,
all that's childlike,
so close to flowers and trees and things,

bringing greenness in.

I'd been in this head for seventy years
when a shrink dropped in
and got locked in.

He taps all night on the wall of my skull,
I don't envy him
- my head is grim like Wormwood Scrubs.

With time on his hands he's widely read
- Papillon, The Wooden Horse
tunnels and things
and his favourite novel's The Great Escape,
his hero the Birdman of Alcatraz,

and he believes my head is the Chateau D'If
and never stops digging, though we're lifers in the head we're in.

OUT & ABOUT WITH MARY

Shopping with Mary

Shopping I hate.
Always puts me in a mood,
but yesterday to keep the peace I went with Mary to Debenham's
and we looked at materials: silks and cottons
and tried things on.
And then I felt a mood coming on
but managed, I think, to keep it hidden -
when, all of a sudden a white rhinoceros ran amok
(one of those from the Serengeti)
smashing Royal Doulton, Wedgewood ware,
knackered knickers panty hose
rampaged, snorted scattered shoppers.
In seconds no one was left in the store
except, of course, Mary and me.
'Keep perfectly still,' Mary said
and we eyed the pachiderm thundering past.
Mary, I noticed, closed her eyes
- I've known her meditate anywhere.
Anyway the beast slowed down and finally stopped,
nibbled ties and socks and lingerie
and Mary approached it confident, calm
and stroked its nose.
'It's tension,' she said patting his head.
'He'll feel much better if we take him out.'

She tied a ribbon round his horn and led him out.
I quietly followed a pace behind.

Hippo

We were walking along the river one day
Mary and I,
a little beyond the railway bridge
when we encountered a hippo drying off.
Mary, excited, ran across
and from her pendulous bag
she drew a measuring tape and lump of sugar
which she offered to the ungulate
artio dactyl - species African.
(Mary classified everything.)

Then she counted its teeth
and mounting its back measured its length from tail to snout,
and then its girth.
Drawing the tape beneath its belly
she paused and listened
- the ruminant rumbled
and breaking wind it tousled the grass as a helicopter might in taking off.
I lost my hat.

Mary, of course, all clinical said
'A hippo a day can supply enough gas
for the needs of an average family of four.'
Then she gave it a mint
which the beast acknowledged with a generous deposit.

'In African rivers,
the chain of life depends on it,' Mary said.
Mary is a specialist in many things.

Wildebeest

On Clifton Ings that day
Mary poked a cowpat with a stick.

'Wildebeest, love.'
'No, cows,' I said.
'Wildebeest, love.'
'Bullshit,' I said
and strode ahead

- a thousand horse flies rose from the cowpats,
over Overton rising dust.

'Wildebeest, love.'

I stomped ahead.

Then, suddenly the Ings was the Serengeti
and a thousand thousand thunderous hooves
shuddered the ground on Richter 10
and day turned to night in a hail of mud
and everywhere snorting, stench and steaming
- a bull thumped the ground
shit splattered my head

and in the tumult Mary's voice:
'It's their annual migration, love.'

And they kept on coming, wave after wave
bumping and jostling, slipping and sliding.

'Keep down, keep down,' Mary said.

I thought the migration would never end.

And then I heard the stragglers drumming a three legged rhythm
and opened my eyes to a gloom of dust
and Mary on her feet already
commentating on their crossing across the Ouse to Poppleton.
'They've crossed the Atavanga Ouse,' she said

Africa shimmered.

From Overton a breeze got up
- mountainous clouds,
drops of rain.

We walked to Skelton, Mary and I.
'A tiger lives in Skelton Copse,' Mary said

'I .. I .. know,' I said.

Mary's Canary

Mary had a bird she taught to sing
arpeggios, trills and scales and things.
She kept it in a gilded cage.

It practised on its own sometimes
but preferably with Mary.

The neighbours grimaced as they passed
and arias poured through keyholes, cracks.

Their forte was fortissimo.

Apart from Clementi, Scarlatti, Bach
to train the bird Mary used osmosis too
and by the cage throughout the night
kept 'The Lark Ascending' on.

I've known them hang on notes so long
you'd think they'd never let them go.

They climbed chromatics and sang duets,
and every night to calm the bird
Mary draped her linen print of English flora over the cage
then came to bed still chirping, singing.

I covered her head.

Tracking the elusive elephants with Mary at night in the City of York

'Tonight we're going on safari, love,' Mary said,
'there're elephants in York though rarely seen,'
and she placed a topee on my head
and strapped a camera to my back, tripod and all.

'We'll follow their droppings love,' she said
'the fresher the better - giant size and steaming hot,
- a sign the quarry is not far off.'
So we scoured Tang Hall and down to town
and at the Lord Mayor's Mansion steps
'I've found one love,' I said, 'I think,' feeling proud.
It was huge like the bowls on the Bert Keech green
but in one word my zeal dried up,
'Dessicated,' Mary said and poked it with a stick
delivering a lecture on how a dropping is like a clock
its lack of surface sheen tells us the time the beast moved off.
In Parliament street I found another
and one in the Shambles and Lord Mayor's walk,
steam rising in the chilly night
'Also apply the texture test,' Mary said.
'Poke it with a stick. If it sticks to the stick, it's fresh,' she said.
'It sticks,' I said. 'Excreta fraiche,' Mary said.
The excreta mounds, bountiful in deposition,
described a circle round the city
and we analysed and classified according to gender and elephant size.
Then Mary read the question in my head:
'Why are elephants rarely seen yet all these droppings?'
'It's their camouflage my love,' she said.
'They pass through at night and merge with the greyness
- Yorkshire mists and Norman stone
so tracking is a way of seeing shapes in shadows, subtle greys'
and we followed the droppings down to the river,
and by the bridge in the shifting mists,
'They're there,' she said,
'tusks glinting in the Northern moon,
squirting the waters of the Ouse.'

The Whale, Crystal Therapy and Mary

One morning we were walking along the river
Mary and I
looking for a picnic spot
when, on a sandy bank we encountered a whale,
beached and bothered in the warming air.
To keep it moist
Mary straightway dowsed the beast
with water from her ice-cold pack
and mounting his back
took from her bag a crystal on a piece of string.
'To calm him down,' she said rotating it over the mammal's head
and I, not knowing what to do paced up and down
stroked his belly then his chin
when, above my head the whirr of crystal on a piece of string.
I stood stone still.
Then the whale it blinked and twitched its tail
and the ground it throbbed beneath my feet
and submerged to the gunnels a barge slipped by
massively pushing the Ouse before it.
Mary smiled
and smeared the whale from head to tail
with Tesco's Virgin Olive Oil
which she blessed with basil and maple leaves,
the dregs she poured upon the sand
in a kind of druidical libatory rite
greasing a slipway for the whale

and the foaming waves rushed up the beach
'Push,' she said and we pushed together and launched the beast
and in the process I launched myself.
The whale expelled a thankful sigh,
spouting a fountain ten feet high
and I, squirting mouthfuls of the oozy Ouse
crawled from the water and flopped on the sand,
above my head the whirr of crystal on a piece of string.

Crocodile

We were walking in the Museum Gardens
Mary and I
when something rustled, large and long
in the Everglades down by the river.
'Genus Crocodilus,' Mary said,
'Order Crocodilia,
they've settled in parks throughout the city.'
Mary's an expert on reptilia.

Then first a nose
and then full length
he stretched before us on the path,
his eyes like glass.
His mouth was open ominous-wide
and Mary popped a sweet inside.
Then starling-size, a bird swooped down
and cleaned his teeth.
'Pluvianus aegyptius,' Mary said.

Then she sang a song
and charmed the beast
and stroked his head.
Entranced,
he was a sculpture of himself.

I gaped inside the cavernous mouth,
pluvianus aegyptius hovered above.

For Christmas Mary bought me a didgeridoo
she also bought me a kangaroo
to improve my jumping.
So we practise jumping on the Ings,
Mary me and the kangaroo.
Last week together we leapt the Ouse
and there's no leap like the kangaroo's
- its grace and skill
though Mary has style
but as for me, I'm not as spry as I used to be
and to mount the air I flap my arms and run full throttle
which the kangaroo would never do.

Oh that I were a kangaroo!
We'd jump around the world together
from Clifton Green to Katmandu,
but tomorrow's our debut in the City of York
- crowds already outside the Dean Court
to see us three
Mary me and the kangaroo
leap the Minster Towers together,
but I wish there weren't this ballyhoo,
we could leap the Minster with less ado
just for friends who
all day long would jump and sing
with Mary me and the kangaroo
and in the dream time late at night
I'd charm them with my didgeridoo.